Key Stage 2 Maths

Standard 15 Minute Tests

TESTBOOK **2**

Dr Stephen C Curran
with Autumn McMahon

Edited by Katrina MacKay

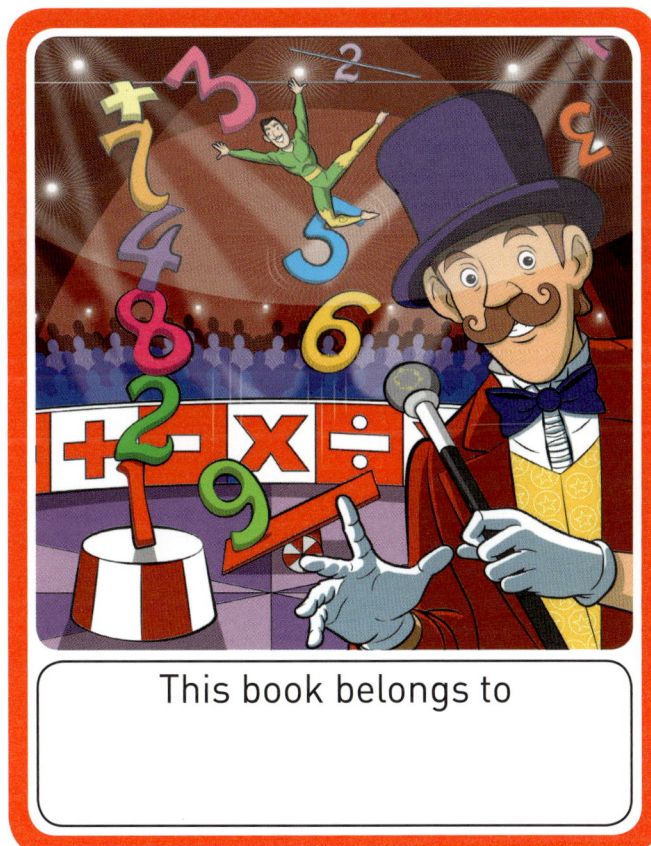

This book belongs to

Accelerated Education Publications Ltd

Do your workings on this page

Mark to %	
0	0%
1	7%
2	13%
3	20%
4	27%
5	33%
6	40%
7	47%
8	53%
9	60%
10	67%
11	73%
12	80%
13	87%
14	93%
15	100%

Maths Test 1

1) Which of the following are prime numbers? _____

16, 10, 3, 31, 4

2) Put these numbers in order, starting with the smallest.

$\frac{7}{8}$ $\frac{1}{2}$ $\frac{3}{4}$ _____

3) Write **12** hours as a fraction of the total amount of hours in a day. _____

4) What is the sum of 2^2 and 3^2? _____

5) Calculate **25%** of **640**. _____

6) $(3 \times 7) + 25 - 16 =$ ____

7) The pie chart shows the choices of favourite colour made by a class of year 4 children. If there are **48** children in the class, how many chose blue? _____

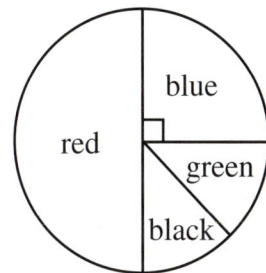

8) Find $\frac{1}{9}$ of **9,180**. _____

9) What is the average of **9, 16, 41** and **30**? _____

10) What is **19** more than **399**? _____

11) Round **216** to the nearest **10**. _____

12) What is the product of **6** and **3**? _____

13) What is the value of angle x? _____

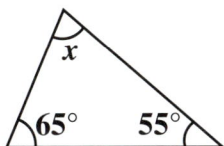

14) A film lasts **2** hours and **45** minutes. If Manjit and Manoj finish watching the film at **23:30**, what time did it start? Write your answer in 12-hour clock. _____

15) 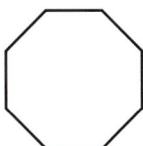 What is this shape? _____

Score [ ] Percentage [%]

Do your workings on this page

Mark to %	
0	0%
1	7%
2	13%
3	20%
4	27%
5	33%
6	40%
7	47%
8	53%
9	60%
10	67%
11	73%
12	80%
13	87%
14	93%
15	100%

Maths Test 2

1) How many sets of parallel sides does this shape have? ____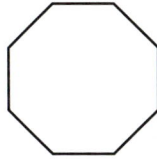

2) Is this true?
8 × 4 + 6 > 45
_____

3) What is the next number?
63, 31, 15, 7, _____

4) How many obtuse angles are there in this shape? _____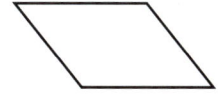

5) **12 + (11 × 10) =** _____

6) **8$\overline{)97}$ = ___ rem ___**

7) What is the sum of the first **3** prime numbers? _____

8) How many vertices does a cuboid have? _____

9) Round **17.55** to the nearest whole number. _____

10) How many axes of symmetry does a hexagon have? _____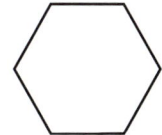

11) What fraction of this shape is shaded? _____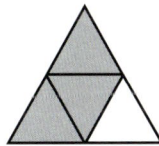

12) What is the sum of the prime numbers from **26** to **42**? _____

13) Ruth's watch is **10** minutes fast. Her watch said **8.53am** when she arrived at school after a **23** minute journey. What was the real time when she left her house? _____am

14) Suresh thought of a number. He added **15**, divided by **3**, then multiplied by **7**. He was left with **49**. What number did he start with? _____

15) What is the lowest common multiple of **12** and **36**? _____

Score [ ] Percentage [%]

Do your workings on this page

Mark to %	
0	0%
1	7%
2	13%
3	20%
4	27%
5	33%
6	40%
7	47%
8	53%
9	60%
10	67%
11	73%
12	80%
13	87%
14	93%
15	100%

Maths Test 3

1) **28** is the product of **7** and **4**. What is the product of **9** and **11**? _____

2) How many faces does this square-based pyramid have? _____

3) What is the missing number?

   68, 51, ___, 17

4) Which number is a factor of both **88** and **33** (do not include **1**)? _____

5) How many acute angles does this drawing have? _____

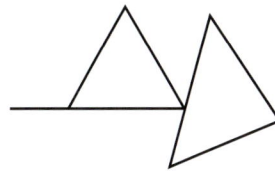

6) A digital clock says **09:23**. How many minutes is it to **10 o'clock**? _____

7) Write these in order of size, beginning with the smallest.
   $1\frac{1}{10}$ $2\frac{2}{5}$ $\frac{3}{4}$ _____

8) **5.4 =** ____ tenths

9) What is the product of **7** and **8**? _____

10) Which is the largest?
    $1\frac{1}{2}$ **1.8** $1\frac{3}{4}$ **2.4** _____

11) Round **54** to the nearest **ten**. _____

12) Angle **A** in this trapezium is _____ .
    (acute, a right angle, obtuse)

13) $1.4 = 1.0 + \frac{4}{?}$ ____

14) Write **20** minutes to **7** in the evening in figures, using am or pm. _____

15) A bowl holds **2** beakerfuls. A beaker holds **4** cupfuls. How many cupfuls will fill **5** bowls? _____

Score [ ] Percentage [%]

Do your workings on this page

Mark to %	
0	0%
1	7%
2	13%
3	20%
4	27%
5	33%
6	40%
7	47%
8	53%
9	60%
10	67%
11	73%
12	80%
13	87%
14	93%
15	100%

Maths Test 4

1) Write, in figures, the number that is **78** more than **three thousand**. _____

2) $1\frac{2}{5} = \frac{?}{5}$ _____ Convert to an improper fraction.

3) $2 = \frac{?}{11}$ _____

4) What is **12** more than **12 × 5**? _____

5) If even numbers are **2, 4, 6**, etc. and odd numbers are **1, 3, 5**, etc., what is the sum of the even numbers between **7** and **13**? _____

6) What is $\frac{3}{4}$ of **16**? _____

7) Find the average of **7, 11** and **15**. _____

8) Place in order, starting with the smallest. $\quad \frac{3}{8} \quad \frac{1}{4} \quad 1\frac{1}{2}$ _____

9) Which number is a factor of both **15** and **27** (exclude 1)? _____

10) What is the next number? **8, 21, 34,** _____

11) If you divide **63** by a number the answer is **7**. What is the number? _____

12) Cans are wrapped in packs of **8**. How many packs are needed for **64** cans? _____

13) Subtract **39** from **92**. _____

14) Find the sum of the odd numbers between **6** and **14**. _____

15) Write **three minutes after 12** in the morning in figures, using am or pm. _____

Score [ ] Percentage [%]

Do your workings on this page

Mark to %	
0	0%
1	7%
2	13%
3	20%
4	27%
5	33%
6	40%
7	47%
8	53%
9	60%
10	67%
11	73%
12	80%
13	87%
14	93%
15	100%

Maths Test 5

1) Which is an odd number? _____

17, 24, 12, 36

2) What is the average of

15, 16 and 20? _____

3) What is half of the difference between 36 and 12? _____

4) This shape is a

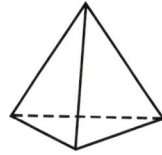

_____
_____ .

(square-based pyramid, triangular prism, tetrahedron)

5) A common factor of 8 and 12 is 4. Find a common factor of 28 and 49 (exclude 1). _____

6) What number is halfway between 11 and 25? _____

7) What is 687 rounded to the nearest ten? _____

8) How many acute angles are there in this triangle? _____

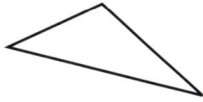

9) Write fifteen minutes to 7 in the morning in figures, using am or pm. _____

10) What is the next number?

145, 136, 127, 118, _____

11) What is the lowest common multiple of 8 and 12? _____

12) $5 = \frac{50}{?}$

_____

13) Chocolates are packed in boxes of 12. How many boxes are needed for 84 chocolates? _____

14) Name the common factors of 14 and 28 (exclude 1).

_____, _____ and _____

15) What is the value of Z? _____

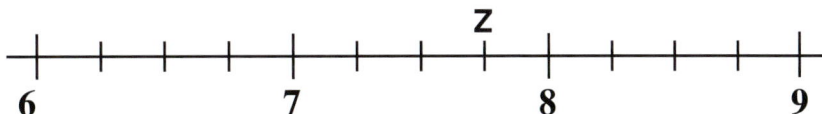

Score [ ] Percentage [%]

Do your workings on this page

Mark to %	
0	0%
1	7%
2	13%
3	20%
4	27%
5	33%
6	40%
7	47%
8	53%
9	60%
10	67%
11	73%
12	80%
13	87%
14	93%
15	100%

Maths Test 6

1) This shape is a _____ .
(rhombus, parallelogram, kite)

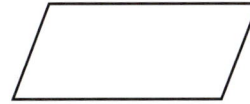

2) Find the average of **34**, **42**, **28** and **16**.
_____

3) Put in order beginning with the smallest: **0.10 0.11 0.01**
_____

4) **6.8** = _____ tenths

5) $\frac{3}{10}$ = **0.3**   Write **0.8** as a fraction in lowest terms. _____

6) What number is at **X**? _____

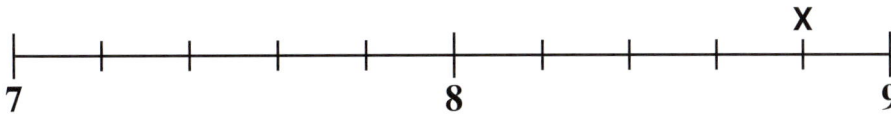

7) If two odd numbers are added together, is the answer even or odd? _____

8) What are the next two numbers?

6, **18**, **30**, ____, ____

9) Round **7.869** to the nearest whole number. _____

10) A pack of sweets contains **9** sweets. There are **12** packs in a box. How many sweets are in one box? _____

11) What is **two** times the difference between **42** and **29**? _____

12) What is the highest common factor of **7** and **14**? _____

13) $\frac{3}{4} + \frac{1}{8}$ = ___

14) What is the product of **6** and **9**? _____

15) A digital clock says **09:48**.
How many minutes is it to **10 o'clock**? _____

Score [ ] Percentage [ ] %

Do your workings on this page

Mark to %	
0	0%
1	7%
2	13%
3	20%
4	27%
5	33%
6	40%
7	47%
8	53%
9	60%
10	67%
11	73%
12	80%
13	87%
14	93%
15	100%

Maths Test 7

1) How many acute angles are there in this drawing?

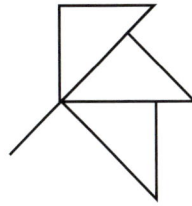

_____

2) Round **999** to the nearest **10**.

_____

3) Is this triangle equilateral, scalene, isosceles or right angled?

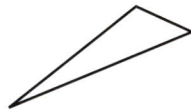

_____

4) Write **4 minutes past 1** in the afternoon in figures, using am or pm.

_____

5) How many vertices does a triangular prism have? _____

6) Put in order starting with the smallest. **2.1**, **2.01**, **2.015**, **2.2**

_____

7) What is the product of **7** and **4**? _____

8) Wendy, Suzanne and Nicole shared **27** sweets equally. How many did they each receive? _____

9) $\frac{6}{24} = \frac{1}{?}$ _____

10) Find the average of **28**, **32**, **30** and **54**. _____

11) What shape is a tissue box? _____ (cuboid, sphere, pyramid, rectangle)

12) What is the value of **A**? _____

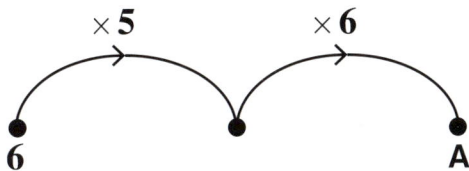

$\times 5$ $\times 6$

6   A

13) What are the factors of **9**?

_____

14) Find the sum of **3²** and **4²**?

_____

15) Which diagram is the odd one out? _____

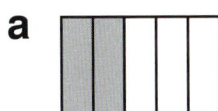

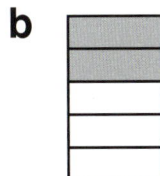

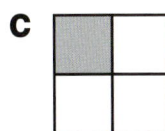

a   b   c   d

Score _____ Percentage _____ %

Do your workings on this page

Mark to %	
0	0%
1	7%
2	13%
3	20%
4	27%
5	33%
6	40%
7	47%
8	53%
9	60%
10	67%
11	73%
12	80%
13	87%
14	93%
15	100%

Maths Test 8

1) Draw a dot pattern to show **10** is a triangular number.

2) There are **18** chocolates in $\frac{3}{4}$ of a box. How many chocolates are in a whole box? _____

3)

Dogs	卌 卌 |||
Cats	卌 卌	
Rabbits	|||
Fish	卌 卌 卌 |||
Other	||
None	**?**

If **50** students took part in a survey about their pets, how many students do not have pets? _____

4) Round **7.483** to the nearest whole number. _____

5) What are the factors of **42**? _____

6) This pie chart shows a year 4 class's choice of ice cream.
   a) How many children like mint? _____
   b) How many children are there in the class? _____

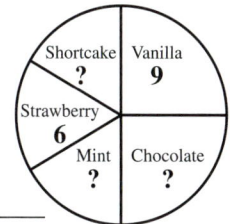

Shortcake ? | Vanilla 9 | Strawberry 6 | Mint ? | Chocolate ?

7) Write **one hundred and seventy-seven thousand, one hundred and forty-four** in figures. _____

8) How many hours are there in **one** week? _____

9) What is **15%** as a fraction in its lowest form? _____

10) If a number is multiplied by **3** and **11** is added, the answer is **20**. What is the number? _____

11) If **24th November** is a Tuesday, what day is the **6th December**? _____

12) What is this shape?

_____

13) What is **2.36pm** on a 24-hour clock? _____

14) Reduce **sixty-seven thousand** by **114**. _____

15) How many minutes are there in $3\frac{1}{2}$ hours? _____

Score ☐ Percentage ☐ %

ae © 2016 Stephen Curran

Do your workings on this page

Mark to %	
0	0%
1	7%
2	13%
3	20%
4	27%
5	33%
6	40%
7	47%
8	53%
9	60%
10	67%
11	73%
12	80%
13	87%
14	93%
15	100%

Maths Test 9

1) Is **91** divisible by **7**? _____

2) $26 - (3 \times 4) =$ _____

3) What is the product of **8** and **9**? _____

4) Write **one million, six hundred and twenty-four thousand, eight hundred and three** in figures. _____

5) What number is halfway between **18** and **42**? _____

6) A number multiplied by itself makes a square number, e.g. $3 \times 3 = 9$. What is the first square number over **10**? ____

7) How many tenths are in **4.7**? _____

8) Jade was born in **1996**. How old was she in **2015**? _____

9) Which letters are symmetrical? **A C F J** _____

10) The floor in a room is _____ . (horizontal, vertical, diagonal)

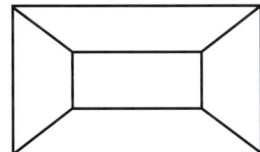

11) Write **60%** as a fraction in its lowest form. _____

12) $x + 13 = 19$ What is the value of x? _____

13) What is the largest number that can be made by arranging the digits **9, 0, 6, 7, 8, 2**? _____

14) Which of these is a prime number? _____
79, 49, 16, 32, 39

15) Write **25 past 9pm** in 24-hour clock. _____

Score [ ]   Percentage [%]

Do your workings on this page

Mark to %	
0	0%
1	7%
2	13%
3	20%
4	27%
5	33%
6	40%
7	47%
8	53%
9	60%
10	67%
11	73%
12	80%
13	87%
14	93%
15	100%

Maths Test 10

1) What number is halfway between **32** and **18**? _____

2) What are the factors of this rectangular number?

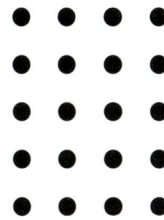

_____

3) What shape can this net make? _____

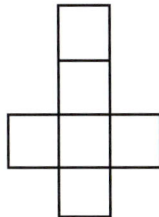

4) The lines in this magic square add up to the same number in all directions. What are the values of **A** and **B**?

A		8
11		B
6	5	10

A = _____   **B** = _____

5) How many triangles can be seen in this drawing? _____

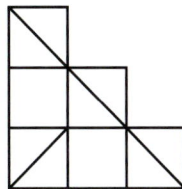

6) Write **1.3** as a fraction or a mixed number.

_____

7) **114 ÷ 8 =** _____ rem. _____

8) **13 + (7 × 4) = (6 × 3) +** _____

9) **51 > 18 + (2 × 7)** Is this true? _____

10) Which is the largest number?
0.8 0.79 0.801 _____

11) 6 $\overline{\phantom{\text{_____}}}$ **14 rem 4**

12) What is the lowest common multiple of **7** and **14**? _____

13)

+2   ×3

A   18

What is the value of **A**? _____

14) Draw a dot pattern to show **15** is a triangular number.

15) What is the value of angle x? _____

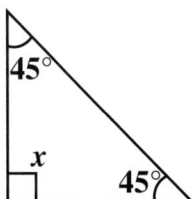

45°

x

45°

Score _____   Percentage _____ %

Do your workings on this page

Mark to %	
0	0%
1	7%
2	13%
3	20%
4	27%
5	33%
6	40%
7	47%
8	53%
9	60%
10	67%
11	73%
12	80%
13	87%
14	93%
15	100%

Maths Test 11

1) What number is at **Y**? _____

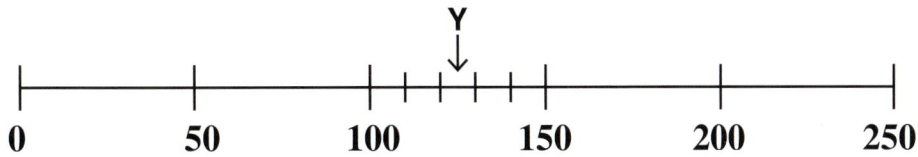

```
0        50        100     150     200     250
```

2) **4²** means **4 × 4.**   **4² = 16**
   What is **6²**? _____

3) $x - 25 = 26$
   What is the value of x? _____

4) What is the smallest number that can be made by arranging the digits **9, 1, 3, 6, 4**? _____

5) **5** and **2** are a pair of factors of **10**.
   Name a pair of factors of **36**. _____ and _____

6) Hannah thinks of a number, multiplies it by **nine** and adds **3**.
   If the answer is **30**, what number did she think of? _____

7) How many obtuse angles are there in this diagram? _____

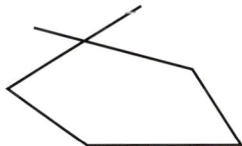

8) Which number is even? _____
   2,015, 1,016, 3,099, 121

9) Megan's dad is **three** times her age. If Megan is **18**, how old is her dad? _____

10) Is **13** a rectangular number? _____

11) What fraction of this shape is shaded? _____

12) What is the total number of days in the months beginning with A? _____

13) $4.2 = 4 + \frac{1}{?}$ _____

14) What shape can be made from this net?

_____

15) Double **260** and deduct **15**. _____

Score [ ]   Percentage [%]

Do your workings on this page

Mark to %	
0	0%
1	7%
2	13%
3	20%
4	27%
5	33%
6	40%
7	47%
8	53%
9	60%
10	67%
11	73%
12	80%
13	87%
14	93%
15	100%

Maths Test 12

1) The lines in this magic square add up to the same number in all directions. What is the value of **A**? _____

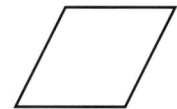

		6
	A	7
4	9	2

2) What number is halfway between **25** and **49**? _____

3) How many diagonal lines are there in this drawing? _____

4) How many lines of symmetry does this shape have? _____

5)  What is the value of **Z**? _____

4 ×6 +8 Z

6) Give two factors of **28**. _____ and _____

7) Round **88** to the nearest **10**. _____

8) Deduct **18** from **41**. _____

9) Find the average of **28**, **13** and **16**. _____

10) What is the next number?
2, 4, 8, 16, _____

11) Which of the following is a square number? _____
30, 17, 24, 26, 49

12) What is the highest common factor of **36** and **27**? _____

13) **18** cans fit into a box. How many cans fit into **4** boxes? _____

14) Write, in figures, the number that is **six** less than **1,800**. _____

15) **0.68 × 10 =** _____

Score _____ Percentage _____ %

Do your workings on this page

Mark to %	
0	0%
1	7%
2	13%
3	20%
4	27%
5	33%
6	40%
7	47%
8	53%
9	60%
10	67%
11	73%
12	80%
13	87%
14	93%
15	100%

Maths Test 13

1) Write **four minutes to one pm** in 24-hour clock. _____

2) How many tenths are there in **7.01**? _____

3) Which angle is acute? _____

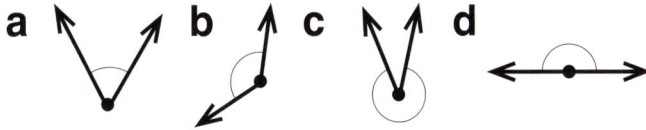

4) What shape is this?

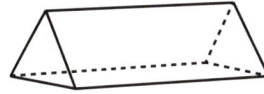

_____

5) Write **75%** as a fraction in its lowest form. _____

6) What number is at **X**? _____

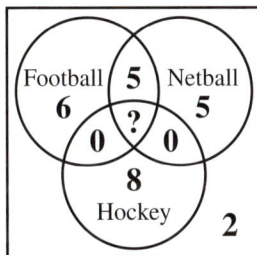

7) Put in order from smallest to largest.

$$\frac{5}{8} \quad \frac{3}{4} \quad \frac{1}{2}$$

_____

8)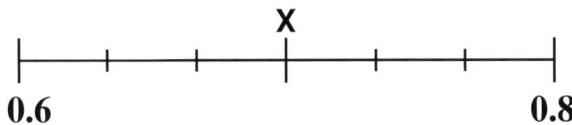

30 students took part in a survey of their favourite sports.

What number is represented by the question mark? _____

9) If the **25th November** is a Friday, on what day does Christmas day fall? _____

November						
M	T	W	T	F	S	S
14	15	16	17	18	19	20
21	22	23	24	25	26	27

10) What is the sum of **42** and **36**? _____

11) What are two factors of **63**? _____

12) A ladder is leaning against a wall as shown. Is the ladder diagonal, parallel or perpendicular? _____

13) What is double the difference between **16** and **32**? _____

14) Write **thirty-two point one** in figures. _____

15) How many lines of symmetry does this shape have? _____

Score [   ] Percentage [%]

Do your workings on this page

Mark to %	
0	0%
1	7%
2	13%
3	20%
4	27%
5	33%
6	40%
7	47%
8	53%
9	60%
10	67%
11	73%
12	80%
13	87%
14	93%
15	100%

Maths Test 14

1) $\frac{4}{4}$ = _____

2) $7 \times (2 + 3)$ = _____

3) Write **2.4** as an improper fraction. _____

4) $4^2 + 3^2$ = _____

5) What is the sum of all the prime numbers between **12** and **20**? _____

6) How many days are there from **13th May** to **16th June**? _____

7) Is **16** a triangular number? _____

8) What is the product of **7** and **3**? _____

9) A school did a survey of students' lunch choices.

Hot school lunches	⊮⊮⊮
Packed lunch	⊮⊮⁞⁞
Salad	⊮⁞⁞⁞

How many students took part in the survey? _____

10) $x - 9 = 25$ What is the value of x? _____

11) What is the lowest common multiple of **6** and **8**? _____

12) What is **20%** of **80**? _____

13) What number is halfway between **16** and **22**? _____

14) Is angle a acute, obtuse or reflex? _____

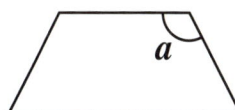

15) Round **72** to the nearest **10**. _____

Score [   ] Percentage [%]

Do your workings on this page

Mark to %	
0	0%
1	7%
2	13%
3	20%
4	27%
5	33%
6	40%
7	47%
8	53%
9	60%
10	67%
11	73%
12	80%
13	87%
14	93%
15	100%

Maths Test 15

1) Is **25** a square, prime or triangular number? _____

2) What is the average of **12**, **16** and **14**? _____

3) Round **0.806** to the nearest integer. _____

4) **18,243 ÷ 10 =** _____

5) If an odd number is added to an even number, is the answer odd or even? _____

6) A TV show started at **6.35pm** and finished at **8.15pm**. How many minutes was it on for? _____

7) How many right angles are there in this drawing? _____

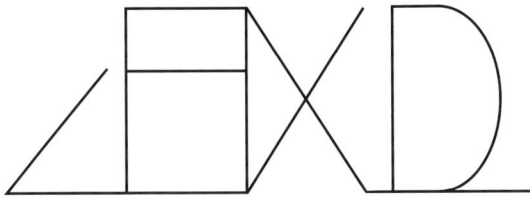

8) Draw a dot pattern to show **6** is a triangular number.

9) What is the next prime number after **7**? _____

10) **11 × 12 =** _____

11) The length of a swimming pool is **7m**. If Milad swims **15** lengths, how far did he swim? _____

12) What is the next number?

1, 4, 9, 16, ____

13) Is this statement true? _____

16 ÷ 4 = 16 − (8 ÷ 2)

14) Which is the largest number? _____

1,972   1,765   2,318   2,381

15) Which angle is reflex? _____

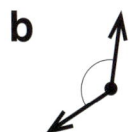

a   b   c   d

 Score [ ] Percentage

 [ ] %

Do your workings on this page

Mark to %	
0	0%
1	7%
2	13%
3	20%
4	27%
5	33%
6	40%
7	47%
8	53%
9	60%
10	67%
11	73%
12	80%
13	87%
14	93%
15	100%

Maths Test 16

1) $76 - (3 \times 12) = (4 \times 12) - 8$

   Is this true? _____

2) What is the next number?

   1, 2, 4, 8, _____

3) How many minutes are there in $2\frac{1}{3}$ hours? _____

4) What is the average of **26**, **16** and **15**? _____

5) Which of the following shapes does not contain any right angles? _____

   a [ ] b c d

6) Helen, Sinead, Maeve and Edel spend an average of **£10** each. Helen spends **£15.60**, Sinead spends **£12.80** and Maeve spends **£6.30**. How much does Edel spend? _____

7) Which angle is a right angle? _____

   a b c d

8) Write **one hundred and twenty thousand and sixty-eight** in figures. _____

9) Round **13.479** to the nearest whole number. _____

10) **5** and **3** are a factor pair of **15**. Give a factor pair of **44**. _____

11) Put these in order, largest first. $\frac{1}{2}$ $\frac{1}{4}$ $\frac{3}{8}$ _____

12) What number is halfway between **16** and **30**? _____

13) How many tenths are there in **3.8**? _____

14) Which two lines are parallel? _____

15) $128 \div 8 =$ _____

Score [ ] Percentage [%]

Do your workings on this page

Mark to %	
0	0%
1	7%
2	13%
3	20%
4	27%
5	33%
6	40%
7	47%
8	53%
9	60%
10	67%
11	73%
12	80%
13	87%
14	93%
15	100%

Maths Test 17

1) Steve's digital watch says **08:50**. If he needs to catch a bus at **09:16**, how long does he have to wait? _____

2) $6^2 - 4^2 =$ ____

3) Sanjay can fit **360** words on a page. How many words can he fit on **3** pages? _____

4) What is the **4th** prime number? _____

5) $x - 11 = 13$
   What is the value of x? _____

6) What is the largest number that can be made by arranging the digits **3, 6, 5, 2, 8**? _____

7) What is the size of angle x? _____

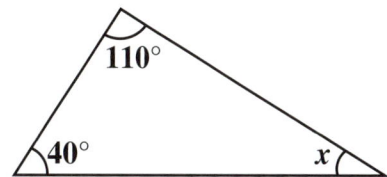

8) $16 \times 3 =$ _____

9) Deduct **13** from **27**. _____

10) What is **30%** of **60**? _____

11) $\frac{3}{10} + \frac{4}{5} =$ _____

12) Which of the following is an odd number? _____
    416, 330, 629, 524, 966

13) What are the factors of **49**? _____

14) What fraction of the shape is shaded? _____

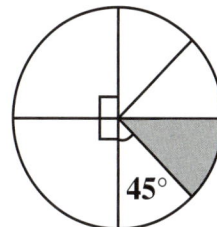

15) Double **36** and add **six**. _____

Score [ ] Percentage [%]

Do your workings on this page

Mark to %	
0	0%
1	7%
2	13%
3	20%
4	27%
5	33%
6	40%
7	47%
8	53%
9	60%
10	67%
11	73%
12	80%
13	87%
14	93%
15	100%

Maths Test 18

1) Write $\frac{7}{10}$ as a decimal. _____

2) What is the lowest common multiple of **6** and **9**? _____

3) $(20 \times 3) + 16 =$ _____

4) What is the value of **Z**? _____

$$3 \xrightarrow{+6} \quad \xrightarrow{\times 7} Z$$

5) All directions add up to the same amount. What is the value of **A**? _____

	5	A
6	1	8

6) Bottles are sold in packs of **12**. If **72** bottles are required, how many packs need to be bought? _____

7) How many hundredths are there in **1.49**? _____

8) Which is the odd one out, **M**, **L**, **H** or **F**? _____

9) Draw a dot pattern to show that **21** is a rectangular number.

10) How many lines were used to make this drawing? _____

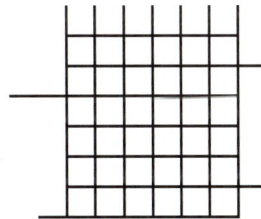

11) What is the smallest number that can be made by arranging the digits **6, 1, 3, 2, 8**? _____

12) **51 > 18 × 3**
Is this true? _____

13) Which of the following is the smallest number? _____
1.016 1.080 1.1 1.006

14) What shape does this net form?
_____

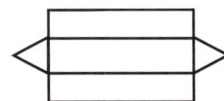

15) Triple **80** and minus **16**. _____

Score [ ] Percentage [%]

Do your workings on this page

Mark to %	
0	0%
1	7%
2	13%
3	20%
4	27%
5	33%
6	40%
7	47%
8	53%
9	60%
10	67%
11	73%
12	80%
13	87%
14	93%
15	100%

Maths Test 19

1) A pantomime starts at **2.40pm** and finishes at **5pm**. What is the duration of the show? _____

2) Draw in the lines of symmetry of this shape.

3) What is $\frac{4}{7}$ of **70**? _____

4) What is **60%** of **35**? _____

5) What is double the difference between **64** and **21**? _____

6) Round **8.15** to the nearest integer. _____

7) What is the value of **9** in **2.94**? _____

8) How many weeks are there in **two** years? _____

9) $17 \times 6 = 13 \times 8$ Is this true? _____

10) Mark needs **90** balloons. The balloons come in packs of **8**. How many packs does he need to buy? _____

11) $6 \times 8 = 8 \times$ _____

12) $132 \div 12 =$ _____

13) The bar chart shows the colours of pencils in a pencil case. How many pencils were there in total? _____

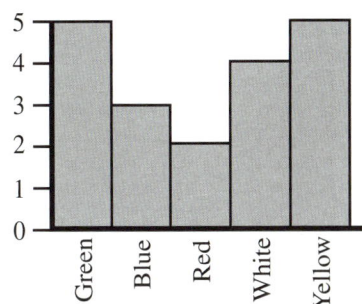

14) What is the name of an eight-sided shape? _____

15) $x + 9 = 17$ What is the value of x? _____

Score [ ] Percentage [%]

Do your workings on this page

Mark to %	
0	0%
1	7%
2	13%
3	20%
4	27%
5	33%
6	40%
7	47%
8	53%
9	60%
10	67%
11	73%
12	80%
13	87%
14	93%
15	100%

Maths Test 20

1) What is the lowest common multiple of **4** and **12**? _____

2) What is the highest common factor of **18** and **45**? _____

3) This pie chart shows the amount of animals on a farm. How many sheep and pigs are there in total? _____

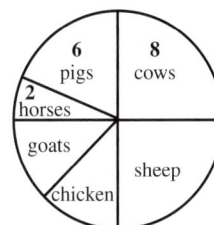

4) What number is halfway between **27** and **39**? _____

5) What is 9×5? _____

6) How many degrees are there in **two** full rotations? _____

7) Write **one minute to midnight** in 24-hour clock. _____

8) If there are **6** delivery drivers and each delivers **22** parcels a day, how many parcels are delivered each day? _____

9) What is the total number of days in June, July and August? _____

10) Which angle is obtuse? _____

11) Which angle is acute? _____

12) What is the average of **22**, **28** and **25**? _____

13) What is the next number?
14, 15, 17, 20, 24, _____

14) Write **one thousand, three hundred and forty-six** in figures.

_____

15) If two odd numbers are added together, is the answer odd or even? _____

Score [   ] Percentage [%]

Do your workings on this page

Mark to %	
0	0%
1	7%
2	13%
3	20%
4	27%
5	33%
6	40%
7	47%
8	53%
9	60%
10	67%
11	73%
12	80%
13	87%
14	93%
15	100%

Maths Test 21

1) What is the average of **16**, **18** and **20**? _____

2) If Sarah needs to get the train at **12:11** and her journey to the station takes **29 minutes**, what time does she need to leave? _____

3) Draw a dot pattern to show that **16** is a rectangular number.

4) If today is **8th November** and Jake has his first school play in exactly **4** weeks, on what date is the play? _____

5) What is the product of **2** and **7**? _____ | 6) **180 ÷ 6 =** _____

7) Write **one thousand and twelve point six** in figures. _____

8) Which three-sided shape has two sides of the same length and two angles the same size? _____ | 9) How many pages will I read if I read **11** pages a day for two weeks? _____

10) How many degrees is it from north to north-east? _____ | 11) What is the value of the **8** in **9.268**? _____

12) What is the value of **Z**? ____ | 13) **(10 × 8) − 14 =** _____

14) What is the greatest number that can be made by arranging the digits **1, 3, 6, 0, 5**? _____

15) Heather leaves her house at **7:56**. She needs to catch the **8:04** bus and her journey to the bus stop takes **7 minutes**. Will she catch her bus? _____

Score [ ]   Percentage [%]

Do your workings on this page

Mark to %	
0	0%
1	7%
2	13%
3	20%
4	27%
5	33%
6	40%
7	47%
8	53%
9	60%
10	67%
11	73%
12	80%
13	87%
14	93%
15	100%

Maths Test 22

1) What number is at **X**? _____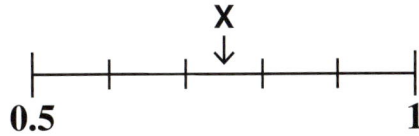

2) Round **923.97** to the nearest **ten**. _____

3) What is the total cost if Teresa spends **£5.83**, Shannon spends **£6.15**, Cheryl spends **£8.16** and Velda spends **£5.97**? _____

4) What is triple **180**? _____

5) If Shane is twice Jamie's age and Jamie is **10**, how old is Shane? _____

6) If **6** fireworks go off per minute, how many fireworks go off in **half** an hour? _____

7) What is **80%** of **120**? _____

8) If a bottle fills **8** glasses, how many bottles are needed to fill **48** glasses? _____

9) What number is double the difference between **61** and **18**? _____

10) $y + 17 = 23$
What is the value of y? ____

11) Which is larger, $\frac{5}{8}$ or $\frac{3}{4}$? _____

12) What is the lowest common multiple of **3** and **9**? ____

13) How many faces (surfaces) does a cube have? _____

14) Which of these numbers is not a prime number?
13, 17, 19, 15, 11 _____

15) Put these fractions in order starting with the largest:

$\frac{1}{2}$ $\frac{3}{4}$ $\frac{7}{8}$ _____

Score [ ] Percentage [%]

Do your workings on this page

Mark to %	
0	0%
1	7%
2	13%
3	20%
4	27%
5	33%
6	40%
7	47%
8	53%
9	60%
10	67%
11	73%
12	80%
13	87%
14	93%
15	100%

Maths Test 23

1) Draw a dot pattern to show that **21** is a triangular number.

2) Double **270**. _____

3) Is this statement true? _____
$(18 \times 3) > (14 \times 4)$

4) What shape is this?

_____

5) Name two factors of **21**.

_____ and _____

6) If Penny's watch is **12** minutes fast and she needs to leave home at **9.28am**, what time will her watch show? _____

7) What is the sum of **21**, **46** and **34**? _____

8) How many lines of symmetry does a regular octagon have? _____

9) Write **50%** as a decimal. _____

10) The legs of a chair are _____ _____ to the seat.
(parallel, perpendicular, horizontal)

11) Is this a scalene, equilateral or isosceles triangle?

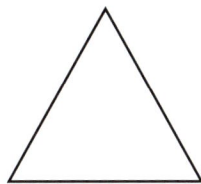

_____

12) What number is half of the difference between **76** and **40**? _____

13) Deduct **6.2** from **7.3**. _____

14) Which of the following is a square number? _____
25 29 27 21 28

15) What date is a fortnight after Christmas Eve?

_____

Score [   ] Percentage [   ] %

Do your workings on this page

Mark to %	
0	0%
1	7%
2	13%
3	20%
4	27%
5	33%
6	40%
7	47%
8	53%
9	60%
10	67%
11	73%
12	80%
13	87%
14	93%
15	100%

Maths Test 24

1) What is the lowest common multiple of **10** and **8**? _____

2) $80 - (10 \times 6) = 4 \times 5$

 Is this true? _____

3) What is the next number?
 1, 1, 2, 3, 5, 8, 13, ___

4) $4 = \dfrac{?}{10}$ _____

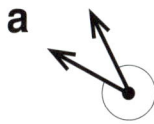 a b 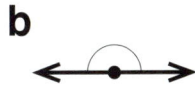 c d

5) Which angle is acute? ___

6) Which angle is obtuse? ___

7) What is the value of the **9** in **7.629**? _____

8) What is the greatest remainder you can have when you divide by **24**? _____

9) What is the smallest number that can be made by arranging the digits **1**, **3**, **8**, **2**, **5**? _____

10) Which is the smallest number?

 $\dfrac{1}{2}$ $\dfrac{2}{5}$ $\dfrac{3}{4}$ _____

11) $16 \times 4 =$ _____

12) $126 \div 3 =$ _____

13) Which of these shapes contain right angles? _____

 F Z M H T

14) What shape does this net form?

 _____

15) Triple **90**. _____

Score [ ] Percentage [ ] %

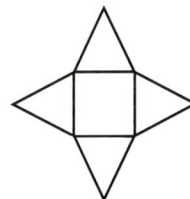

49

Do your workings on this page

Mark to %	
0	0%
1	7%
2	13%
3	20%
4	27%
5	33%
6	40%
7	47%
8	53%
9	60%
10	67%
11	73%
12	80%
13	87%
14	93%
15	100%

Maths Test 25

1) What is the average of **24**, **23** and **31**? _____

2) If a coach can seat **20** people and a class of **53** students and **6** teachers are going on a school trip, how many coaches will they need? _____

3) Write **one thousand, eight hundred and ninety-three** in figures.

_____

4) Round **8.45** to the nearest integer.

_____

5) Put in order, smallest first: $\frac{1}{2}$ $\frac{2}{5}$ $\frac{3}{4}$ _____

6) Which shape is the odd one out?

a   b   c   d   _____

7)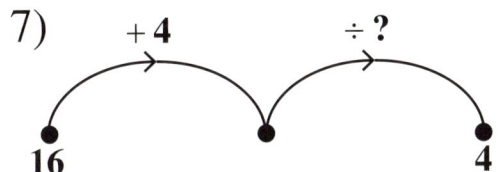

_____

8) Write **5 minutes to eight** in the morning in figures, using am or pm.

_____

9) If it is a leap year and **14th February** is a Tuesday, on what day will **1st March** fall? _____

10) What is the highest common factor of **30** and **42**? _____

11) What number is halfway between **19** and **45**? _____

12) Are the angles inside this rectangle acute, right angles or obtuse? _____

13) Is this true? _____

$18 \times 4 > 24 \times 3$

14) $x - 7 = 13$ What is the value of x? _____

15) If Peter had **ten 20p** coins, **five 50p** coins and **three 10p** coins, how much money did he have in total? _____

Score [ ]   Percentage [%]

Do your workings on this page

Mark to %	
0	0%
1	7%
2	13%
3	20%
4	27%
5	33%
6	40%
7	47%
8	53%
9	60%
10	67%
11	73%
12	80%
13	87%
14	93%
15	100%

Maths Test 26

1) $\frac{1}{4} + \frac{3}{8} =$ _____

2) $(6 \times 12) - (4 \times 3) =$ _____

3) What is the next number?
   1, 2, 5, 10, ____

4) What shape is a can of peas? _____

5) What number is at **X**? _____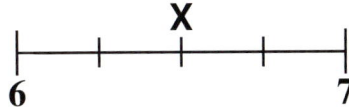

6) How many tenths are there in **8.9**? _____

7) What type of number is **4**? _____
   (square, triangular, prime)

8) $17\overline{)198}$ = ____ rem ____

9) How many horizontal lines are there in this drawing? ____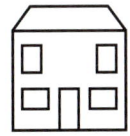

10) What is the next prime number after **19**? _____

11) Deduct **62** from **131**. _____

12) Write **20%** as a fraction in its lowest terms. _____

13) Which number is the largest?
    1.012   1.12   1.0012   1.21   0.112 _____

14) **17** × **4** = _____

15) A film runs for **2** hours **35** minutes, if it starts at **12:40**, at what time will it finish? _____

Score [ ]   Percentage [%]

Do your workings on this page

Mark to %	
0	0%
1	7%
2	13%
3	20%
4	27%
5	33%
6	40%
7	47%
8	53%
9	60%
10	67%
11	73%
12	80%
13	87%
14	93%
15	100%

Maths Test 27

1) What is the lowest common multiple of **3** and **12**? _____

2) What is the highest common factor of **18** and **27**? _____

3) Write **13 minutes to ten** at night in 24-hour clock. _____

4) How many days are there from **25th May** to **27th June**?

_____

5) $(16 \times 3) - 10 > 40$ Is this true? _____

6) What is the average of **24**, **17** and **16**? _____

7) **13** books fit on one shelf. If there are **5** shelves in a bookcase, how many books fit in the bookcase? _____

8) Round **815** to the nearest **10**.

_____

9) Write two factors of **36**.

_____

10) Put in order, largest first: **1,006**, **100.6**, **1,060**, **10.60**

_____

11) What number is halfway between **68** and **46**? _____

12)

13) How many lines of symmetry are there in this shape? ____

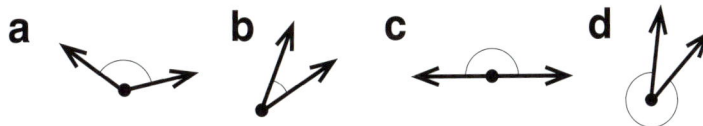

14) Which angle is reflex? ____

15) Which angle is obtuse? ____

Score [ ] Percentage [%]

Do your workings on this page

Mark to %	
0	0%
1	7%
2	13%
3	20%
4	27%
5	33%
6	40%
7	47%
8	53%
9	60%
10	67%
11	73%
12	80%
13	87%
14	93%
15	100%

Maths Test 28

1) What is the missing number?
   48, **40**, **32**, ____, **16**

2) What is the average of
   17, **13**, **5** and **1**? ____

3)

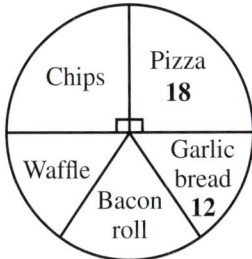

   This pie chart shows the snacks some students bought at lunch. How many students were there in total? _____

4) Write **three hundred and forty-five point seven** in figures. _____

5) There are **20** biscuits in a pack. Jack buys **5** packs. How many biscuits does he buy? _____

6) If an odd number is multiplied by an even number, will the answer be odd or even? _____

7) How many hundredths are in **2.62**? _____

8) Draw a dot pattern to show that **12** is a rectangular number.

9) What is the highest remainder you can have if you divide by **13**? _____

10) The legs of a chair are _____ to each other. (parallel, perpendicular, diagonal)

11) What is the only even prime number? ____

12) What is the total of **15**, **9** and **8**? _____

13) Each line adds up to **15** vertically and horizontally (not diagonally). What number should replace the question mark? ____

	?	9
7		
6	8	1

14) $x + 6 = 24$ What is the value of x? ____

15) How many obtuse angles are there in a regular hexagon? _____

Score ☐   Percentage ☐ %

Do your workings on this page

© 2016 Stephen Curran

Mark to %	
0	0%
1	7%
2	13%
3	20%
4	27%
5	33%
6	40%
7	47%
8	53%
9	60%
10	67%
11	73%
12	80%
13	87%
14	93%
15	100%

Maths Test 29

1) What time would it be **eighteen** minutes after **quarter to nine** in the evening (write in 24-hour clock)? _____

2) $(10 \times 3) - 16 = 7 \times$ _____

3) $\dfrac{7}{10} + \dfrac{63}{100} =$ _____

4) How many minutes are there in **2** hours and **21** minutes? _____

5) Which 3D shape has **5** vertices and **one** square face? _____

6) Round **2,016** to the nearest **10**. _____

7) Give **2** factors of **60**. _____

8) Put in order, largest first. $1\frac{1}{3}$ $1\frac{1}{6}$ $1\frac{4}{5}$ _____

9) What number does **X** represent? _____

X
↓
├┼┼┼┼┼┼┼┼┼┤
0   1

10) Which is the odd one out? **F E H T** _____

11) What is **7** squared? _____

12) This chart shows the varieties of tree a student saw. How many trees did they see altogether? _____

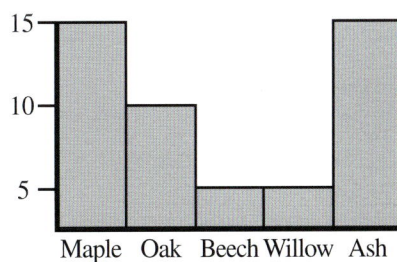

Maple Oak Beech Willow Ash

13) What is the value of **A**? _____

×**6**   ×**3**

2   A

14) How many lines of symmetry does a rhombus have? _____

15) What is $\dfrac{3}{4}$ of **100**? _____

Score [ ] Percentage [%]

Do your workings on this page

Mark to %	
0	0%
1	7%
2	13%
3	20%
4	27%
5	33%
6	40%
7	47%
8	53%
9	60%
10	67%
11	73%
12	80%
13	87%
14	93%
15	100%

Maths Test 30

1) $\frac{1}{2}$ of a number is **40**. What is $\frac{1}{5}$ of the number? _____

2) Is this angle acute, obtuse or reflex? _____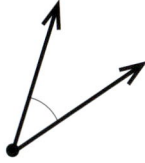

3) Write **nine hundred and twenty-three point six** in figures. _____

4) What is the lowest common multiple of **4** and **8**? _____

5) What is the next number?
1, 7, 13, 19, ___

6) What is the average of **17, 21** and **22**? _____

7) Mr Beaver took his **3** children to the cinema. He paid **£17.40** in total and an adult ticket cost **£7.35**. How much did each child ticket cost? _____

8) Dave is making drinks for **6** people. He puts **2** ice cubes in each drink. How many ice cubes does he use? _____

9) What number is halfway between **16** and **48**? _____

10) What does the **6** represent in **4.627**? _____

11) Is **15** a triangular or square number? _____

12) What is the product of **8** and **8**? _____

13) What is **25%** of **80**? _____

14) What is the greatest number that can be made by arranging the digits **2, 1, 7, 6, 5**? _____

15) Is this true? **1.008 > 1.08** _____

Score [   ]   Percentage [%]

Do your workings on this page

Mark to %	
0	0%
1	7%
2	13%
3	20%
4	27%
5	33%
6	40%
7	47%
8	53%
9	60%
10	67%
11	73%
12	80%
13	87%
14	93%
15	100%

Maths Test 31

1) What time is an hour and a half later than **8.15pm** (write in 12-hour clock)? _____

2) $90 - (8 \times 7) =$ _____

3) How many hours are there in **3** days? _____

4) $3\frac{1}{10} + \frac{3}{10} + \frac{9}{100} = 3.$___

5) How many lines of symmetry are there in this shape? _____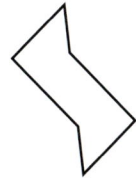

6) **8** books fit in a box and **6** boxes fit on a pallet. How many books fit on one pallet? _____

7) Write **1,672** in words. _____

8) Round **48** to the nearest **ten**. _____

9) Give **2** factors of **48**. _____

10) Divide **128** by **4**. _____

11) $x - 6 = 16$ What is the value of x? ____

12) In a leap year February has **29** days.
A leap year occurs every **4** years: **2008, 2012, 2016**.
Was **1992** a leap year? _____

13) Which is the smallest number? $\frac{1}{2}$, **0.48**, $\frac{3}{5}$ ____

14) $\frac{9}{9} =$ _____

15) Take **8-tenths** from **7.62**. _____

Score [   ]   Percentage [%]

Do your workings on this page

Mark to %	
0	0%
1	7%
2	13%
3	20%
4	27%
5	33%
6	40%
7	47%
8	53%
9	60%
10	67%
11	73%
12	80%
13	87%
14	93%
15	100%

Maths Test 32

1) What is the lowest common multiple of **4** and **6**? _____

2) **23rd** November is Wednesday, what day is **3rd** December? _____

3) Is this true? _____
   1.016 < 1.02

4) What is the average of **48**, **46** and **41**? _____

5) Which shape is a prism: cuboid, cone or pyramid? _____

6) Which angle is reflex? ___

7) Which angle is a right angle? ___

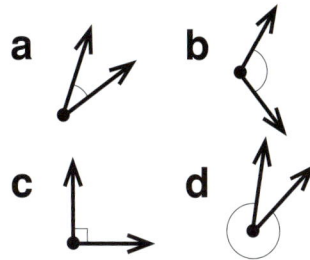

8) Put in order, largest first: $\frac{4}{5}$ **0.7** $\frac{3}{4}$ _____

9) If an odd number is multiplied by an odd number, will the answer be odd or even? _____

10) What is the value of **A**? ____

11) Are the walls in a room vertical, horizontal or diagonal? _____

12) In a class, $\frac{3}{4}$ of the students like apples and the rest like pears. If there are **40** students in the class, how many like pears? _____

13) Which of the following is a prime number? _____
    23, 26, 30, 33, 15

14) What fraction of the shape is shaded?
    _____

15) **12 × 9 =** _____

Score ☐ Percentage ☐ **%**

Do your workings on this page

Mark to %	
0	0%
1	7%
2	13%
3	20%
4	27%
5	33%
6	40%
7	47%
8	53%
9	60%
10	67%
11	73%
12	80%
13	87%
14	93%
15	100%

Maths Test 33

1) $4 = \dfrac{?}{100}$ _____

2) Draw a dot pattern to show **28** is a rectangular number.

3) What is the name of this shape? _____

4) A lesson finishes at **11.45am**. If the classroom clock is **18** minutes slow, what time would it say at the end of the class? _____

5) $\dfrac{3}{8} > \dfrac{1}{4}$ Is this true? _____

6) $40 - (8 \times 5) =$ ____

7) **20** calculators fit in a box. If a school buys **3** boxes, how many calculators did they purchase? _____

8) How many lines of symmetry does a regular pentagon have? _____

9) The rungs of a ladder are _____ to the sides of the ladder. (parallel, perpendicular, horizontal, diagonal)

10) What is the lowest common multiple of **6** and **7**? _____

11) Write **8,624** in words. _____

12) Put in order, largest to smallest. **50% 0.2** $\dfrac{1}{4}$ _____

13) Take **6.2** from **10**. _____

14) How many acute angles are there in this shape? _____

15) Are these lines parallel or perpendicular? _____

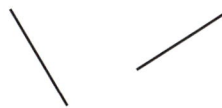

Do your workings on this page

Mark to %	
0	0%
1	7%
2	13%
3	20%
4	27%
5	33%
6	40%
7	47%
8	53%
9	60%
10	67%
11	73%
12	80%
13	87%
14	93%
15	100%

Maths Test 34

1) Draw a dot pattern to show **18** is a rectangular number.

2) Multiply the sum of **6** and **8** by **3**. _____

3) What is the average of **17**, **26** and **11**? _____

4) **6** and **3** are a factor pair of **18**. Give a factor pair of **24**. ____

5) What is the missing number?
   13, **16**, **19**, ___, **25**

6) How many hundredths are in **1.13**? _____

7) Which is a reflex angle? ____
8) Which is an acute angle? ____

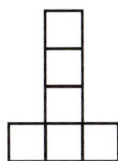

9) $x + 3 = 16$ What is the value of x? ____

10) What shape will this net form? _____

11) **360 ÷ 8 =** _____

12) There are **12** pencils in a pack. An office requires **86** pencils. If **8** packs are bought, will there be enough pencils? _____

13) **12** ⟌ **354** = _____ rem. _____

14) This tally chart shows a group of children's choice of books. How many children were surveyed in total? _____

Genre	Amount of Children
Comedy	⌇⌇⌇ |||
Fantasy	⌇⌇⌇ ⌇⌇⌇ ⌇⌇⌇ ||
Animal	||
Non-fiction	|||

15) How many vertical lines are there in this diagram?

_____

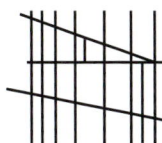

Score [   ] Percentage [**%**]

Do your workings on this page

Mark to %	
0	0%
1	7%
2	13%
3	20%
4	27%
5	33%
6	40%
7	47%
8	53%
9	60%
10	67%
11	73%
12	80%
13	87%
14	93%
15	100%

Maths Test 35

1) Write **two thousand, two hundred and eighty** in figures.

_____

2) How many days are there in total in the months beginning with **J**? _____

3) What is the value of **A**? ____

$\times 2$ $+6$

5   A

4) What is the lowest common multiple of **9** and **12**? _____

5) A school play starts at **6.30pm**. If it lasts for **2** hours **25** minutes, what time will it finish? _____

6) What shape is this? _____

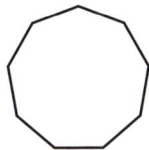

7) What type of angle is this? _____

8) $\frac{1}{5}$ of a number is **40**. What is $\frac{1}{4}$ of the number? _____

9) What number is halfway between **25** and **17**? _____

Each column and row adds up to **18**.

10) What is the value of **A**? _____

11) What is the value of **B**? _____

B	A	9
	11	2
7		7

12) What is **25%** of **60**? _____

13) $\frac{13}{10}$ = __.__

14) What is the value of angle **y**? 50° y

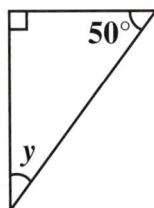

_____

15) What type of triangle is this? _____

Score [   ] Percentage [%]

© 2016 Stephen Curran

71

Do your workings on this page

Mark to %	
0	0%
1	7%
2	13%
3	20%
4	27%
5	33%
6	40%
7	47%
8	53%
9	60%
10	67%
11	73%
12	80%
13	87%
14	93%
15	100%

Maths Test 36

1) How many degrees are there in **5** right angles? _____

2) Write two factors of **22** (exclude **1**). _____

3) What is the product of **9** and **13**? _____

4) What is the lowest number that can be made by arranging the digits **1, 5, 8, 2, 7**? _____

5) What is the average of **21, 12** and **24**? _____

6) What is the next number?
2, 3, 5, 9, ____

7) **38 − (9 × 3) =** ____

8) $\frac{14}{10} = 1\frac{2}{?}$ ___

9) **16** children each paint **2** pictures. If **34** pictures are needed for a display, how many more are needed? _____

10) Which angle is obtuse? ____

11) Which angle is a right angle? ____

 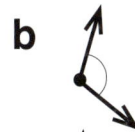 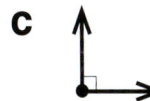

12) Round **1.471** to the nearest unit. _____

13) What is the value of the **3** in **6.326**? _____

14) What type of number is **6**? _____
(prime, square, triangular)

15) 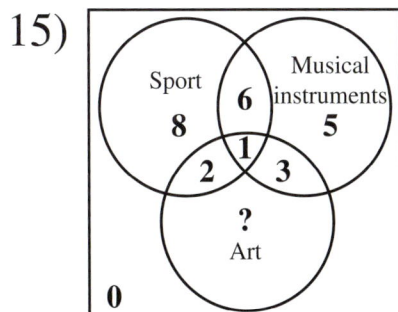 This Venn diagram shows some children's hobbies. If **30** children were surveyed, what number does the question mark represent? _____

Score ⬜ Percentage ⬜ %

Notes

Answers

Test 1
1) 3, 31
2) $\frac{1}{2}$, $\frac{3}{4}$, $\frac{7}{8}$
3) $\frac{1}{2}$
4) 13
5) 160
6) 30
7) 12
8) 1,020
9) 24
10) 418
11) 220
12) 18
13) 60°
14) 8.45pm
15) regular octagon

Test 2
1) 4
2) No
3) 3
4) 2
5) 122
6) 12 rem. 1
7) 10
8) 8
9) 18
10) 6
11) $\frac{3}{4}$
12) 138
13) 8.20am
14) 6
15) 36

Test 3
1) 99
2) 5
3) 34
4) 11
5) 8
6) 37
7) $\frac{3}{4}$, $1\frac{1}{10}$, $2\frac{2}{5}$

8) 54
9) 56
10) 2.4
11) 50
12) acute
13) 10
14) 6.40pm
15) 40

Test 4
1) 3,078
2) 7
3) 22
4) 72
5) 30
6) 12
7) 11
8) $\frac{1}{4}$, $\frac{3}{8}$, $1\frac{1}{2}$
9) 3
10) 47
11) 9
12) 8
13) 53
14) 40
15) 12.03am

Test 5
1) 17
2) 17
3) 12
4) tetrahedron
5) 7
6) 18
7) 690
8) 2
9) 6.45am
10) 109
11) 24
12) 10
13) 7
14) 2, 7, 14
15) 7.75 or $7\frac{3}{4}$

Test 6
1) parallelogram
2) 30
3) 0.01, 0.10, 0.11
4) 68
5) $\frac{4}{5}$
6) $8\frac{4}{5}$ or 8.8
7) even
8) 42, 54
9) 8
10) 108
11) 26
12) 7
13) $\frac{7}{8}$
14) 54
15) 12

Test 7
1) 6
2) 1,000
3) scalene
4) 1.04pm
5) 6
6) 2.01, 2.015, 2.1, 2.2
7) 28
8) 9
9) 4
10) 36
11) cuboid
12) 180
13) 1, 3, 9
14) 25
15) c

Test 8
1) ∴∴ or ∴∴
2) 24
3) 3
4) 7
5) 1, 2, 3, 6, 7, 14, 21, 42

6) a) 6
   b) 36
7) 177,144
8) 168
9) $\frac{3}{20}$
10) 3
11) Sunday
12) cylinder
13) 14:36
14) 66,886
15) 210

Test 9
1) yes
2) 14
3) 72
4) 1,624,803
5) 30
6) 16
7) 47
8) 19
9) A, C
10) horizontal
11) $\frac{3}{5}$
12) 6
13) 987,620
14) 79
15) 21:25

Test 10
1) 25
2) 1, 2, 4, 5, 10, 20
3) cube
4) A = 4 B = 3
5) 11
6) $1\frac{3}{10}$ or $\frac{13}{10}$
7) 14 rem. 2
8) 23
9) yes
10) 0.801
11) 88
12) 14

Answers

13) 4

14)
or

15) 90°

Test 11
1) 125
2) 36
3) 51
4) 13,469
5) 1×36 or 2×18 or 3×12 or 4×9 or 6×6
6) 3
7) 4
8) 1,016
9) 54
10) no
11) $^5/_8$
12) 61
13) 5
14) tetrahedron or triangular-based pyramid
15) 505

Test 12
1) 5
2) 37
3) 7
4) 2
5) 32
6) Two of: 1, 2, 4, 7, 14, 28
7) 90
8) 23
9) 19
10) 32
11) 49

12) 9
13) 72
14) 1,794
15) 6.8

Test 13
1) 12:56
2) 70
3) a
4) triangular prism
5) $^3/_4$
6) 0.7
7) $^1/_2, ^5/_8, ^3/_4$
8) 4
9) Sunday
10) 78
11) Two of: 1, 3, 7, 9, 21, 63
12) diagonal
13) 32
14) 32.1
15) 8

Test 14
1) 1
2) 35
3) $^{12}/_5$
4) 25
5) 49
6) 34
7) no
8) 21
9) 35
10) 34
11) 24
12) 16
13) 19
14) obtuse
15) 70

Test 15
1) square
2) 14

3) 1
4) 1,824.3
5) odd
6) 100
7) 12
8) or
9) 11
10) 132
11) 105m
12) 25
13) no
14) 2,381
15) c

Test 16
1) yes
2) 16
3) 140
4) 19
5) d
6) £5.30
7) d
8) 120,068
9) 13
10) 1×44 or 2×22 or 4×11
11) $^1/_2, ^3/_8, ^1/_4$
12) 23
13) 38
14) a & c
15) 16

Test 17
1) 26 minutes
2) 20
3) 1,080
4) 7
5) 24
6) 86,532
7) 30°
8) 48
9) 14
10) 18

11) $1^1/_{10}$ or $^{11}/_{10}$
12) 629
13) 1, 7, 49
14) $^1/_8$
15) 78

Test 18
1) 0.7
2) 18
3) 76
4) 63
5) 3
6) 6
7) 149
8) M
9)
10) 14
11) 12,368
12) no
13) 1.006
14) triangular prism
15) 224

Test 19
1) 2 hours 20 minutes or 140 minutes
2)
3) 40
4) 21
5) 86
6) 8
7) 9-tenths or 0.9 or $^9/_{10}$
8) 104
9) no
10) 12
11) 6
12) 11
13) 19

Answers

14) octagon
15) 8

Test 20
1) 12
2) 9
3) 14
4) 33
5) 45
6) 720°
7) 23:59
8) 132
9) 92
10) a
11) c
12) 25
13) 29
14) 1,346
15) even

Test 21
1) 18
2) 11:42
3) (dot pattern) or (dot pattern)
4) 6th December
5) 14
6) 30
7) 1,012.6
8) isosceles triangle
9) 154
10) 45°
11) 8-thousandths or 0.008 or $^8/_{1000}$
12) 30
13) 66
14) 65,310
15) yes

Test 22
1) 0.75
2) 920
3) £26.11
4) 540
5) 20
6) 180
7) 96
8) 6
9) 86
10) 6
11) $^3/_4$
12) 9
13) 6
14) 15
15) $^7/_8, ^3/_4, ^1/_2$

Test 23
1) (dot pattern) or (dot pattern)
2) 540
3) no
4) rhombus
5) Two of: 1, 3, 7, 21
6) 9.40am
7) 101
8) 8
9) 0.5
10) perpendicular
11) equilateral
12) 18
13) 1.1
14) 25
15) 7th January

Test 24
1) 40
2) yes
3) 21
4) 40
5) c
6) d
7) 9-thousandths or 0.009 or $^9/_{1000}$
8) 23
9) 12,358
10) $^2/_5$
11) 64
12) 42
13) F, H, T
14) square-based pyramid
15) 270

Test 25
1) 26
2) 3
3) 1,893
4) 8
5) $^2/_5, ^1/_2, ^3/_4$
6) d
7) 5
8) 7.55am
9) Thursday
10) 6
11) 32
12) right angles
13) no
14) 20
15) £4.80

Test 26
1) $^5/_8$
2) 60
3) 17
4) cylinder
5) 6.5
6) 89
7) square
8) 11 rem 11
9) 12
10) 23
11) 69
12) $^1/_5$
13) 1.21
14) 68
15) 15:15 or 3.15pm

Test 27
1) 12
2) 9
3) 21:47
4) 33
5) no
6) 19
7) 65
8) 820
9) Two of: 1, 2, 3, 4, 6, 9, 12, 18, 36
10) 1,060, 1,006, 100.6, 10.60
11) 57
12) 3
13) 5
14) d
15) a

Test 28
1) 24
2) 9
3) 72
4) 345.7
5) 100
6) even
7) 262
8) (dot pattern) or (dot pattern)
9) 12
10) parallel
11) 2
12) 32
13) 4

Answers

14) 18
15) 6

Test 29
1) 21:03
2) 2
3) $1\frac{33}{100}$ or $\frac{133}{100}$
4) 141 minutes
5) square-based pyramid
6) 2,020
7) Two of: 1, 2, 3, 4, 5, 6, 10, 12, 15, 20, 30, 60
8) $1\frac{4}{5}$, $1\frac{1}{3}$, $1\frac{1}{6}$
9) 0.8
10) F
11) 49
12) 50
13) 36
14) 2
15) 75

Test 30
1) 16
2) acute
3) 923.6
4) 8
5) 25
6) 20
7) £3.35
8) 12
9) 32
10) 6-tenths or 0.6 or $\frac{6}{10}$
11) triangular
12) 64
13) 20
14) 76,521
15) no

Test 31
1) 9.45pm
2) 34

3) 72
4) 49
5) 0
6) 48
7) one thousand, six hundred and seventy-two
8) 50
9) Two of: 1, 2, 3, 4, 6, 8, 12, 16, 24, 48
10) 32
11) 22
12) yes
13) 0.48
14) 1
15) 6.82

Test 32
1) 12
2) Saturday
3) yes
4) 45
5) cuboid
6) d
7) c
8) $\frac{4}{5}$, $\frac{3}{4}$, 0.7
9) odd
10) 3
11) vertical
12) 10
13) 23
14) $\frac{4}{7}$
15) 108

Test 33
1) 400
2) or
3) regular heptagon

4) 11.27am
5) yes
6) 0
7) 60
8) 5
9) perpendicular
10) 42
11) eight thousand, six hundred and twenty-four
12) 50%, $\frac{1}{4}$, 0.2
13) 3.8
14) 2
15) perpendicular

Test 34
1) or
2) 42
3) 18
4) 1×24 or 2×12 or 3×8 or 4×6
5) 22
6) 113
7) b
8) a
9) 13
10) cube
11) 45
12) yes
13) 29 rem. 6
14) 30
15) 9

Test 35
1) 2,280
2) 92
3) 16
4) 36

5) 8.55pm or 20:55
6) regular nonagon
7) obtuse
8) 50
9) 21
10) 3
11) 6
12) 15
13) 1.3
14) 40°
15) isosceles

Test 36
1) 450°
2) Two of: 2, 11, 22
3) 117
4) 12,578
5) 19
6) 17
7) 11
8) 5
9) 2
10) b
11) c
12) 1
13) 3-tenths or 0.3 or $\frac{3}{10}$
14) triangular
15) 5

PROGRESS CHARTS

Test	Mark	%
1		
2		
3		
4		
5		
6		
7		
8		
9		
10		
11		
12		
13		
14		
15		
16		
17		
18		

Test	Mark	%
19		
20		
21		
22		
23		
24		
25		
26		
27		
28		
29		
30		
31		
32		
33		
34		
35		
36		

CERTIFICATE OF

ACHIEVEMENT

This certifies

_____

has successfully completed

Key Stage 2 Maths
Year 4/5
TESTBOOK **2**

Overall percentage
score achieved

%

Comment _____

_____

Signed _____

(teacher/parent/guardian)

Date _____